What Diamonds Can Do

What Diamonds Can Do

Poems by Claire Keyes

Cherry Grove Collections

Published by Cherry Grove Collections
P.O. Box 541106
Cincinnati, OH 45254-1106

ISBN: 9781625491282
LCCN: 2015934761

Poetry Editor: Kevin Walzer
Business Editor: Lori Jareo

Visit us on the web at www.cherry-grove.com

Cover design: Kristi Donahue
Cover photo: Janice Koskey

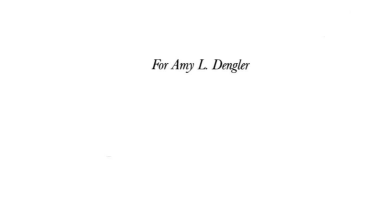

For Amy L. Dengler

Acknowledgments

With thanks to the editors of the following journals where these poems have appeared, sometimes in previous versions or with different titles.

Adanna: "You Should Avoid Young Children"

Blast Furnace: "Icarus on the Empire State," "Where I Am the Girl in the Backyard Photo"

The Common: "What Diamonds Can Do"

Common Ground Review: "On the Blue Line"

Conclave Journal: "The Moth Man"

Crab Orchard Review: "Long Branch, New Jersey"

Honeyland Review: "After Giselle "

In A Gilded Frame (anthology): "Angelus"

Innisfree Poetry Journal: "Atalanta, or the Audacity of Speed"

The Ledge: "Castle Valley, Utah"

Literary Bohemian: "Talus"

Northwoods Journal: "Winter Visit to the D. H. Lawrence Ranch"

Oberon: "Swamp Willow," "Poem in Which Many Plates Are Broken," "Phragmites," "Why the Fishermen of Newfoundland Shoot Icebergs"

Of Sun and Sand (anthology): "Einstein at the Beach," "Kayaking the Sakonnet"

Rockhurst Review: "Buddha-Lips"

Sugar Mule: "Winter Beach with Gibbous Moon," "Bosque del Apache," "The Blue Tent," "The Sounds Loneliness Makes"

Tattoo Highway: "The Dodge in the Woods," "Self-Portrait with Bell's Palsy," "The Wisdom of Crows"

Theodate: "Gospel Sing, Key West"

Umbrella Journal: "Blame the Birches," "The Midas Touch"

Verse Wisconsin: "Lines for the Girl in the Blue Jacket," "Night Crossing," "Augury"

womenwriters.net: "R. Crumb at the Grand Canyon," "The Day Pavarotti Died"

Thanks also to my friends in writing: Judith Black, Susanna Brougham, Michelle Gillett, Priscilla Herrington, Jacquelyn Malone, Betsy Morris, Mary Jane Mulholland, Dawn Paul, J. D. Scrimgeour, Carol Seitchik, Pat Sylvia and Suellen Wedmore.

Contents

One

Lose Something Every Day

Poem in Which Many Plates Are Broken

Santorini, 2003

Armies massed for the invasion of Iraq
and a tremble of fear across the region
fail to deter us as we gather inside a taverna
in Santorini. Didn't we sail into its caldera,
finding a harbor at the foot of precipitous cliffs?

Perched on top, a town tracing its heritage
to Minoan Crete, a taverna, percussive music,
even a Zorba in his workman shoes and dark pants.
He rises from his table to join three men stooped over
two guitars, a bouzouki. There's heaviness in his feet
and legs as he dances the hunger of his life, slowly
spinning, turned by forces outside his control.

He is Achilles, desolation in his hero-heart:
his beloved friend slain. Terrible loss travels
through his trunk and limbs, his feet attacking the floor,
the music turning him faster and faster until we think
he must break. Achilles broke, his heart touched
by Priam's grief over his son murdered and defiled.
Something moved in the depths of the hero
and Achilles reached out.

Our dancer gestures, white handkerchief unfurled:
come, join. We surprise ourselves, rising
to place a hand on a shoulder, like comfort—or trouble,
everyone forming the line that winds in and out,
everyone connected although we don't notice it
most of the time, as if what's happening in your soul,
your country could have nothing to do with travelers
who watch aghast as waiters fling plates onto the floor
and they shatter, fragments flying.

Augury

In the flow of traffic, I follow the drama
of red-winged blackbirds harassing a crow,
that sacker of nests. How splendid the torment
as they dart in low above the marshes
to peck his rump.

I slow down, shift to the right lane, following
the scuffling birds as if they were an augury
Homer would describe in assiduous detail:
how they foretell his hero's destiny, the clash
between peoples, Troy reduced to a smoldering ruin.

Blackbirds flash scarlet epaulets; the crow banks and turns,
flummoxed. A truck looms up, blocking my view.

It's the summer of the rig exploding
in the Gulf of Mexico, of pelicans and turtles
coated with sludge, flames shooting into the sky,
the ocean coursed by rivers of oil and beaches blackened
by wave after wave of this man-made mess.

And still I drive.

We live dangerously. Drive dangerously.
I want to stop the car, get out and follow the blackbirds,
find out what they know
about the sanctity of nests.

The Sounds Loneliness Makes

Not that he needed to tell us he was lonely.
Not that he wasn't welcome to use the bedroom
that was my brother's grown up, enlisted.
But those nights I'd lie awake
hearing Uncle Red's footsteps as he climbed the stairs.
Was he drunk again? Then the thud of his shoes
as he dropped them, the fierce wooziness
of his snores.

Childless, he had been fatherly
when all we knew of father was distance. Giving
when all we knew was stricture. Summers,
he drove us to the beach, one arm on the wheel,
the other edging towards Aunt Jo's knee, stopping
for the hair of the dog that bit him.

So I never said anything of my fear
that he would push open my door, fall on top of my bed.
Thinking, I don't know what.
To protect him? To protect myself from saying?
Then he didn't come home. One night, two:
found in an alley in the South End.

My father identified his body at the morgue.
No sounds
when he got home. Just the tightness of his jaw,
a look that said, *Don't ask.*

Streetscape

When gods walked the earth
in the guise of beggars, tramps were safe,
tramps were holy. Come, sit close by the fire,
eat of this lamb roasting on the coals.
Is that light we see reflected in your eyes
Helios himself taking the measure
of our hospitality?

No gods here in Salem, just street people,
caps pulled over their ears, collars turned up
on the rarest days in June. Not even Alan Bates
in that French movie walking bare-assed down the street
just men who urinate in the parking garage stair-well.
A winter ago, park benches slicked with ice,
one used the dumpster behind "Bill and Bob's
Roast Beef" for a bed, spending the night cuddled up
in the trash, his body a stiff curl like the corpse I found once,
a yellow jacket in the silled begonia.

A man hugs the edge of the sidewalk, the side
closest to inside, as if he might fall off
if he came too close to the curb, losing
whatever he carries in the bag swinging from his fist.
I skirt him, make sure not to draw his attention, provoke
his curse, or his spit. Leaving him to trudge behind,
I hear his babble. Is he Athena in the guise of Mentor,
ready with the best of advice? Is she
with the shopping bags, lovely Artemis
skillful in running?

Solitary Walker

No day is ever too hot, too cold,
no block too slippery from recent snows
to interrupt your walk.

Warm days produce two of you: the morning walker
in his white T-shirt and cut-offs and his afternoon twin
in gray T-shirt and cut-offs.

But it's just *Billie,* the guys on the block call you.
You're the handyman I see painting trim on houses, cleaning trash
from yards, mowing lawns.

There's something suspect about you.
Maybe a crime that means you can never drive,
never get too close to children?

At the least, you're simple of mind,
your loneliness overt—and scary, your trek
like my recurring dream of walking the streets downtown,

searching for the car I've parked and misplaced,
making wrong turns, my quest endless,
maddening. And the next day, every day,

there you are, pushing through our streets.
From the safe surround of my porch, I wave to you.
You wave back.

R. Crumb at the Grand Canyon

He comes out of the Men's Room, short
and folded in on himself and I know him
by his scruffy dark beard, by the crush hat
he wears against the Arizona sun.

Like every cartoon of him you've ever seen, he's pale.
Can you imagine R. Crumb sunning? Beside him,
his wife, the equally short and younger Aline,
adjusting her hair, wind-blown. Behind thick glasses,
his eyes scan the motley crowd of tourists
before he heads for the canyon, its fabulous crests
and stark plunges drawing the eye
a mile or more down to the copper-brown river.

Its brutality attracts him: some big ditch.
Brutal in his own way, he never flinches
from depicting his flaccid body and pocked face,
whiskers to scare children.

The canyon wears its scars with élan.
Over time they translate into beauty.
Beside it, celebrity is a moment's interest,
then reduced, like everything else,
to a pip.

Blame the Birches

How could webworms resist
their slender green shapes and copious leaves:

a summer's banquet.

Nature is slovenly
 in spawning moths, offering our trees

for their dismal feast.
We die a little each day.

Lest we forget, nature sends moths, worms,
boils, tumors.

When it starts to drizzle
we move inside,

the hokey mirror pinned on the wall
receiving our images:

Look sharp!

we're cautioned as over our shoulders,
the wind snaps the trees

and the silken tents shiver.

Where I Am the Girl in the Backyard Photo

A girl in a cotton dress
sits on a kitchen chair, posed by her sister
with her knees clamped, her ankles crossed,
only a thin layer of dust between her and eternity.

Moths have eaten the secret
behind her smile. What else she should leave
to the moths: how to sit, how to stand and wait.

Decades pass and she visits her sister,
slumped over in her wheelchair.
At eighty-five, she weighs one pound
for each of her years, wanting to leave this life
and wanting to stay. She can't hear, only feel.
One son hates her other son. She hides her chagrin.

Her mother is my mother. Her father, mine,
but we're little more than strangers.
I lean towards her and brush my lips
across her cheek. She smiles.
There are no more secrets
only the knowledge that one will pass
though the gate before the other.

Only that nothing will remain
but a wrinkled photo: a backyard,
a chair, a girl in a cotton dress.

The Dodge in the Woods

When we pass a car junked beside the trail,
I imagine a dead body festering in the trunk
and feel a spike of fear.

Oh come on, my husband says,
it's just a Dodge.

He turns back to check it out, reminding me
that country people ditch cars all the time:
in their front yards, the woods.

Get a few guys, a couple of six packs, flip it over.

He kicks it.
A worthless shit-box of a car, this Dodge.

A coupe with swept wings,
nothing can camouflage its pathos: no joy rides,
no agile lovers wrestling in its back seat.

In the lee of its bruised fender, seedlings
root and stretch towards the sun.
Soon a forest growing up
and through the car—as in the Yucatan,
the Mayan ruins.

The Dodge sinks
further into the earth. He's gone on
and I hustle to keep up.

Black Friday

for Jdimytai Damour

I can't stand this, he mutters to his buddy on the line
trying to hold back a crush of people
pressing against the sliding glass doors.
He means more than the number of shoppers
waiting all night for the DVDs, the flat-panel TVs,
the video games.

He means the rapacious eyes, the lips mouthing curses,
the sign *Blitz Line Forms Here,*
as if Wal-Mart were a football field
and he and his pals called up to play defense.

He means the assumption that because he's a big man—
270 pounds—and black that he enjoys being pressed
into this security job. He should have called in sick.
His mom in Haiti this Thanksgiving
meant dinner at his sister's house
before coming to work: roast turkey, oyster stuffing,
his niece crawling onto his lap and reaching up
to pull his dreadlocks.

As the doors shatter, he trips and falls.

On TV, late-comers denounce the *savages*
who trampled him to death. Someone heard a man scream,
I've been in line since yesterday morning,
the muddle around the body beyond infuriating.

Local Woman Missing, Locked Car Found on Shore Drive

She left no note, her shopping trip
ordinary as Egg Rock on the horizon.
Her husband escaped every morning, didn't he?
And she pretended to sleep, delaying the change
from nightgown to street clothes:
what street, who to visit?

She watches a jogger
until he's a spot on the beach.
She hasn't run since she was a girl,
yet something pounds inside her.
She has no words for it,
but she's never felt so present,
so entranced at the face that stares back
from the side window: a mouth
she can twist into a smile.

Rolling down the window, she sniffs
the rank odor of algae. It reminds her
of cabbages ripened and unpicked in their garden
among shallow-rooted clover and celandine, weeds
she refused to pluck out. She takes pleasure in fruit
left to rot in the refrigerator beside leftovers
in plastic wrap, their blooms a luminous blue.
What dinner, who to feed? She slips off
her pumps, pulls on her son's old running shoes.

He will search the towns to find her locked car
and never know why she was drawn to this shore.
She knew no one would notice: children
still in school, most runners tied up at noon.
And when she hardly casts a shadow,
she will run towards the water, slowly at first,

then stepping boldly onto the front page,
first a headline, then page two,
then a smudge on the fingers, an ache
that won't go away.

Castle Valley, Utah

We came here for respite and found neighborly mule deer
passing lightly between desert sage
and flowering juniper.
Bats wheel out of caves at nightfall
and the dead keep watch from slits in canyon walls.
The Valley of the Kings is younger than this.
The cliff face shifts its aged flank
sending a rock slide tumbling down canyon walls.

When I lift my glasses
to crenellated cliff-tops I catch a peregrine falcon
raiding a magpie's nest, the lesser bird attacking the marauder
and sending it caterwauling to the mesa.
The yapping of dogs begins at moonrise
as if they too felt something alien and inimical: those spirits
making a circuit around our house, pretending
they are moon-shadows.

This valley creates its own laws, shaped by eons of stark erosion:
volcanic cones
smoothed and wasted
by millennia of wind-blown sand,
the same sand that roughs my skin and enters my nose and eyes
from this you came
           to this you will return.

Swamp Willow

Two men buttressed by a truck, a chipper attached
like a cranky caboose, take down the swamp willow.

Air-borne, one man wields his chain-saw
from a bucket dangerously close to utility wires.

The other feeds the tree, chunk by chunk
into the machine that chews them up

then shoots the chips into the maw of the truck.
The men work hard, cutting, lifting, shredding.

My willow won't cradle the moon, nor shadow
the October yard, daisies spent, asters on the ascent.

After an hour's hacking, the forked stump stands topless,
a remnant that opens up a space I'm not sure I can fill.

Once branches embraced the sky, roots stretched deep
into the past century.

The tree man commiserates, telling me
it was rotting away: ants, fungus.

Lose something every day, Elizabeth Bishop tells herself
as if she needed to practice, as if we could develop

a flair for loss.

Why the Fishermen of Newfoundland Shoot Icebergs

At a desolate port, a fishing boat waits
like a clerk who hasn't seen a customer all day.
Fish all but gone, they're game

for a tourist or two. My husband stands on the prow
alert for sea birds, his passion; mine, the iceberg
we've seen from shore.

It's cold enough, even in July,
for me to huddle down below with captain and crew.
I sit on a foot locker

while the boat tosses and heaves along the coast,
rain spitting against the glass wind screen.
When an iceberg visits, the captain says,

fishermen gather up their rifles and shoot.
His mate expounds: *Icebergs snarl nets.*
A few bullets open a crack,

splitting the ice to hasten its melting.
I meet my husband on deck when we draw close
to the mountain of ice, its ridges and crevasses

monumental. Air pockets reflect the light
which glows green as emerald, a vast beauty
rivaling the dawn sky which has spread

measureless and pink ever since the north Atlantic
thrashed with the great nation of Cod.
But no more, the fishermen's rage rising
with their rifles, taking aim and raking the sky

as if determined to become
a presence no one can ignore.

After Giselle

In the crowded trolley, I feel someone touching me,
a man gesturing to the seat he's vacated, asking,

Would you like to sit down?

His voice is hesitant and even though I'm stiff
from three hours folded into a balcony seat at the ballet,

I'd rather stand and take pleasure
in the swaying of the car and the vision of myself

performing an arabesque, my right leg elevated,
toe pointed back

while my left leg steadies and supports the line of my body
parallel to the floor.

For my back is limber, had better be
after all my sun salutations, my vinyasas.

And here's this man.

The look in his eyes, like I'm his beloved granny.
Is he twenty, twenty-five?

He sees not a prima ballerina, but a woman of a certain age.
I'd like to slug him, blacken his clueless eyes.

Still, there's his gallantry, rare as Raleigh's cape

here in Boston on the Green Line in the twenty-first century.
So I thank him and sit down.

Elizabeth at the Window, 1603

Her reflection, a wraith
in a white nightgown, dares
pity her white hair, her lips
drawn and silent.

Bed would come later.
Much later.

Her chamber: her dying room.
When she was ready.

No make-up, no wig,
damp wisps of hair clinging to her neck,
she looks beyond
her reflection, mirrors
banished long ago.

The Spanish Armada scattered
in the breath of God's wind.
The triumph. The rejoicing:
to be loved
by so many, loved by no One.

She'd outfoxed them: greedy
of marriage proposals, wary
of husbands, childbirth.

So they deemed her the *Virgin Queen*.
A myth, but useful.

Still, her successor: Mary's child.
James, King of Scotland,
to rule her England?

Grim, a secret Catholic, trouble.

I am tied, she bursts out. *I—am tied.*
This tightness in her neck,
this macabre swelling.

Helpers guide her
to cushions on the floor,
someone saying
she *must* sit, fingers
on her shoulders, pressing her elbow.

The word 'must,' she commands,
    is not to be used to Princes.

The Wisdom of Crows

A nurse tapes my wedding ring to my finger.
So it won't come loose, she says,

but I know it's something more
suspect and recall my aunt in the nursing home,

her rings lifted, counterfeits taking their place.

and I know why the nurse wears plastic gloves
before handling the syringe

and taping the IV to my arm.
It drips sucrose and sedative into my purged body,

my curly intestine so clean
the surgeon can snip a polyp

like a chrysanthemum or a tulip.

In the recovery room, I listen
as hammers strike walls, renovating.

I prop myself up and watch crows
through tall windows. They glide from tree to tree,

bleak couriers of survival.

When this is over, I'll plant bulbs.
I'll dig deep and bury them, then pray

for a long, cold winter,
a thick blanket of snow.

Winter Beach with Gibbous Moon

We need the beach this March day,
for the pungent rot of seaweed mixed with the elixir
of brine. For the seagull's gambit, heading off, a crab in its beak,
another gull zooming up with a shriek.
We need rocky outcrops that defy the Atlantic's thrust and pull,
beatings they've taken for millennia.

And it's not just us, crazy to exit the winter house.
Midway, a loon forages. We recognize the migrant's head,
his distinctive white necktie, and listen for the weirdness of his call.
Riding the surf close to shore, sea geese rise in concert
with one another, fall, then rise again, winter guests
more beautiful than their name.

Brant, you call them.

The moon, with a notch in its side, haunts the day,
measuring our months with cold imprecision.
Surfers don't care what month it is.
And we need their distant figures
timing a wave's best surge, pointing their boards,
then riding the curl.

Two

The Labyrinth

The Midas Touch

In that brief moment
after her father's kiss
she must have felt cold
all over, yet brilliant
and hardened to the tears
of the man who wept
at her feet.

In the muffler shop
I fan myself
with last month's *Time*
waiting to be called
by the receptionist,
her fingertips
flashing crimson,
this job of hers
no match
for the proud arch
of her eyebrows.

I don't know who
she thinks she is
or why Midas thought
he was such hot stuff
the gods would not do him dirt.

And what do we remember?
Not a fool
brought low,
but the magic
of his touch.

Wellington Station

It's a new station. That's my excuse.
When I exit the train, damned if I know
which way to my car. Wherever most people
are headed, I decide, into a weird walkway
long as a dragon's tail. *I don't remember this,* I think,
but my body keeps walking like the fool
who persists in her folly.

As often as I've entered the labyrinth
in my dreams, following the slightest thread,
through the darkest door, I'm still strung out
to find myself alone at night in a place both strange
and familiar. At the end of the passage, a man
sits behind plate glass with one small hole in it.
Surely he will recognize my parking ticket
and point me to my car.

That's not one of ours, he says and shrugs.

I turn around and take the passageway in reverse.
Fewer people now, a single woman far ahead
who must register the slap of my footsteps as panic
or danger. She turns her head, steals a look.
As I pass, I almost hear a sigh of relief.
A sign reads: *Buses and Parking Lot* and there,
my car sits, indifferent.

So I didn't plan well.
So my lapses cause chagrin.
In myself, this labyrinth.

Lines for the Girl in the Blue Jacket

My back turned on the plate glass windows
plastered with ads, the July sun thrown away
on the supermarket parking lot, I'm the girl
in the blue jacket, drawing vegetables
off the conveyer belt, right hand fingers striking
the keys, the heel of my palm hitting Add.
Ca-chung! shoving them behind to join the Cheerios
and Spam. *Ca-chung!*

I've no time to envy tanned boys and girls
jostling at the express check-out with their chips
and six packs. How am I to know Saturday
means filling the cooler with beer and sandwiches,
motoring to the boat on the club launch,
raising the sails?

My world is cheeky bag boys, milk spilled
on the conveyer belt, clunky steel carriages
and a friend I race to see how much cash
we can take in.

Some Saturday afternoons, my fingers smudged
by all the bills shuffled and turned, I gaze
after the head cashier, longing for him
to press in behind me, to take the bundles
of fives, tens, twenties, for our hands to touch,
drudgery transformed by desire

On the Blue Line

A young black man rests his head against his hand
like a Nubian Adonis, his left arm relaxed
on the railing. His blonde girlfriend scans the newspaper,
lifting it near her face. She must need glasses.
Like all Venuses, she is vain.

A wide span of legs, her man gazes up
at the subway map. She rests her left elbow
on his right thigh, delicately.

Doors open, shut. Other people rise, walk off.
She folds the paper, then places her hand on his thigh,
leaning her lovely head towards him.
He nuzzles it with his chin. She moves her head
onto his shoulder, their gestures so intimate
yet so public they might be lovers in a film.

When I close my eyes, they fade
and in their guises that couple in Franklin Park,
years ago, strolling by, hand in hand, until
our friend Paul, a man for whom I yearned
with all the ardor of my virgin heart, howled
a racist slur. How the filth emerged
from his gorgeous mouth I'll never know,
but the air was filled with his hate, the rock
in his hand threatening a brawl, so the rest of us,
appalled and horrified, held him back,
the couple fleeing.

Until today on the Blue Line, in a long, agonizing
dissolve, Venus and Adonis take their place.

What Diamonds Can Do

Some write poetry on glass windows
like Sophia Hawthorne at the Old Manse
with her wedding ring. Common enough
in the nineteenth century, but it was like finding a note
in a bottle picked up on the beach. I felt a kind of awe.

Granted, Sophia was the wife
of you know who and could commit
what is, in essence, graffiti. With no repercussions.
And granted, she must have been godawful bored
when he took off the morning after the snowstorm
to visit Thoreau. And left her alone with the baby.

But still, scratching on the window
of a rented house in the room where his imagination
played with dark things. So like him
to face his desk to the wall. She stood looking out
the window. Snowy fields, icy river.

Was it really just being overwhelmed
by the pretty view, *the trees all glass
chandeliers* as she wrote? After coining
the metaphor, she incised it with gusto.

And like most mothers she had to brag
about her kid, *Una, only ten months old*,
and named for Spenser's *Faerie Queene* heroine.
Did posterity really have to know
she *stood on the window sill?*

So we record the minutia
of our lives, gambling that significance
rests in our homely dramas. Thus Sophia
got down on her knees, diamond in hand,

proud mother, yes, but incidental
not at all, a someone

who signed her name with a flourish.

Icarus on the Empire State Building

photo by Lewis W. Hine

1. The Photo

High above New York City,
his feet twined around a cable
suspended from the Empire State,
Hine's steelworker wears no safety belt
no helmet, nothing
between him and the street
but his muscled arms
all-American good looks
and casual—if posed—bravado.

It's 1931.
Time to raise up the working man.
Who more spectacular?

2. Blue-Collar

I didn't know we were working class
only that my father
wore the blue uniform
of a guard on the MTA
only that he left the house
before anyone else got up
that he walked a mile
to the nearest trolley stop
that he got home earlier
than most fathers
smelling of cigars
and city sweat

that *union* was a sacred word
in our house

like communion
like the Virgin Mary
that a man who crossed picket lines
was a scab
that being a scab
was like wearing the mark of Cain
killing one's brother
akin to taking another man's job

taking the food off
his family's table.

3. Journeyman

And my brothers were blessed
to be invited to join Local 7
the Ironworkers Union
to move up the ladder
from apprentice to journeyman
to full-fledged ironworker

working on high steel
was like nothing else
the danger   the freedom
the skill   the sheer terror
of catching or firing rivets
ten   twenty   thirty stories
up, straddling a beam.

Nothing like that power.

4. My Father's Number One Son.

Hero of World War II
special forces, Normandy: Jim
parachuting behind enemy lines

all the stories—if even half of them
were true

Hero of the high steel
the wound in his gut
worming its way into his soul.

Until then,
    he was high-steel man
    Hine's Icarus incarnate.

5. Myths

Everyone knows
they're not true.
Everyone knows
there's some truth in them
even if the truth
begins in a lie.

Real ironworkers
they're a little wild.

Or a lot wild,
you know?

And they're all hustlers,
        they're all hard workers.

6. Hustler

It's you
isn't it, Jim?
says the neighbor
who has seen Hine's photo
of the handsome young man
in a magazine.

Though he was in knee pants
in '31.
Jim agrees that yes,
that's him

and displays the photo
in his family room
on the wall near the TV.

Girl, Descending

None could see that sales girl taking the backstairs at Macy's,
escaping on a fifteen-minute break from her counter
to a world of concrete walls and tiers of steps,
remote and quiet. For this was her stage,
the handrail her barre
as she thrust herself forward and out,
landing lightly on her feet.

She stretches the jump from four steps to seven or ten,
for her legs are long and an angelic coach attends her:
Bend those knees.
Leap. Extend. Never fall.
Never let the idea of fall enter your head.

I want to get close, very close to her
to capture what if feels like to live without fear,
to listen to the rapid beating of her heart.

She listens to no one
telling her she should know better
than to risk cracking her head open.
All she hears is the satisfying slap of her feet touching down
only to spring up again

and take another flight of stairs, intoxicated
with her freedom: sixteen years old, in the city
at night, working a job, getting paid.

Yet the danger is real, jumping the stairs foolish.
The greater danger: to listen to what they say:
don't put yourself at the top of anything,
don't forget you're a girl.

And still I see that girl jettison herself into space
night after night
landing solidly on her feet.

Buddha-Lips

Green-uniformed soldiers board our train
and stand motionless as terra-cotta legions
buried with Emperor Qin Shi Huang.

We rattle and sway towards Canton.
Tiananmen Square hasn't happened.
The Chinese dragon economy sleeps
coiled around its tail.

I glance at the soldiers,
the crème de la crème of Chinese manhood,
their lips full, shapely and luscious.
Think of being kissed by those lips,
Buddha-lips I didn't expect
on Mao's soldiers.

China moves me like no other country,
not even Ireland. The further from the city we travel
the deeper the shift back in time—one hundred, two
hundred years: oxen pulling plows, children
winnowing grain or shepherding frisky geese.

My ancestors lived like this, humbly,
close to the earth. Not for them, soldier guardians
with fleshy lips, the descendants, perhaps,
of Kublai Khan's soldiers, subjugators
bequeathing lips that never grimace in pain
or hunger.

Confucius says, *Woman who worships Buddha-lips
risks sore trouble.* Sensuous, I insist, but lime-green
uniforms offset them and stiff-brimmed hats
crowning their officious heads.

Abide With Me

Why I sing songs of belief in a personal god
in whom I no longer believe:

for the smile spreading across Virginia's lips
as my friends and I assemble around her death bed
in the nursing home and harmonize
Abide with me

for Virginia, struggling to rise up and sing along with us,
saying as we finish, *so pretty,* looking at each of us
with her wide eyes and generous mouth, *so pretty*

only today there is no rising up, only weariness
and the weight of death pressing upon her

for she can no longer lift her head yet moves her lips
to form the shapes and sounds of the beloved hymn

for death assumes a less disturbing face
around Virginia's bed and irony slips away
like the wooly bear caterpillar finding refuge in the grass

for intellect takes the backseat when empathy drives me
and maybe a smidgen of jealousy: the intense love
for a personal god, displaced god of my childhood

he will usher her to the other side

and what if I don't believe?
her human spirit defies my disbelief

for she, more than any personal god,
is unity and harmony

for no savage beast inhabits her soul
only a joy that spreads and touches the singers
who have come to solace her.

Infantile

What's wrong with children playing hopscotch
on the sidewalk or sledding a hilly open field

between houses? What's wrong with the girl
who lived on the first floor of the triple-decker

owned by the Italians across the street?
Infantile paralysis, they told us.

Sitting like a floppy rag doll in her wheelchair,
she watched us play, her head bobbing, the babble

coming out of her mouth never advancing to speech.
We knew she loved us, but she couldn't color a map,

multiply or skip rope. She could only slobber
and grin at our antics. I waved to her, but never

stepped onto her porch, her flowered robe a shroud
for limbs that floundered against the railings, her hands

jerky. She's a sliver of meaning into childhood,
a She who could never be Us.

Yet it's her cousin I flush to remember: Joe Scopa,
tall, darkly handsome and calm even when we taunted him:

Josefina, please no leana on the bella,
the casual prejudice we didn't know was prejudice

just as we didn't know the heart of a girl who existed
for us, if at all, as a shadow.

Long Branch, New Jersey

Winslow Homer

I regret very much
that I have painted a picture
that requires any description, Winslow Homer replied
to a request. What could be simpler than blue sky,
summer beach? Two ladies stand at the edge of the bluff,
their skirts casting an almond shadow on the grass.
It's not easy being a lady in America in 1869,
one's existence devoted to being above it all.

The one with a raised parasol
looks down at the beach, the waves humming
their impatience to meet the shore. A small white dog
forever pounces towards his mistress. Does the lady in grey
lean on her parasol to savor ocean air or simply to spy
on bathers and beach-walkers? The green swath
on which they stand thrives in defiance
of the wind-eroded bluff, the continent's edge
slipping into the sea.

Behind him, his Civil War assignments—
battlefields, snipers, the cruelly dead.
None of that at Long Branch, just ladies like doves of peace.
How brilliant the bustle on the sands—children, men—
the sun in full summer bloom. Speckled with clouds,
this day may resolve in hasty departures.
For now, no darkness allowed.

Einstein at the Beach, 1945

Poised on a rock, his back towards the harbor, Einstein
in shorts and a polo shirt relaxes for the photographer.

My, what shapely legs he has and those sandals: open-toed
with a strap around his instep, a slight heel. Legs crossed,

he could be Lauren Bacall summoning Bogie for another cigarette.
He is grinning. Surely he doesn't know yet about Hiroshima and
  Nagasaki

only what it's like to be revered and to rue his one great mistake.
I think of him every time I watch the strangely prescient *Fantasia:*

the Sorcerer's Apprentice attempting his Master's tricks:
homely buckets of water turned into a tsunami. Even if Einstein

wanted to contain his theories, tie them up like a packet of letters
shoved to the topmost shelf in the laboratory, he couldn't.

With scientists, that's not how it works: ideas shared, enhanced,
qualified, amended, and once out there made more beautiful.

The beauty of his math, his equations, cast a spell on the rest of us
so we think Einstein a metaphor for genius. He grins at the photographe

enjoying himself this fine day, the war close to its end, relaxing
with friends. Who can blame him? Who knows what burdens

his mind bears, what private hell his heart.

Phragmites

You're right. I should never
have brought home the phragmites
and arranged them in a vase.

I don't know what I was thinking.

Well, I wasn't thinking, to be honest.
I was responding to their height,
their grace, their manner of capturing
the winter light in their plumes,
the way they leaned away from the breeze
then assumed their height again.

They called to me.
I heard the rustling of their reeds,
their dance like the courting ritual
of long-necked cranes. One was not enough.
I must have several. All right, an armful.
The marsh didn't seem to mind.
There were so many, a sea of phragmites.
Only the sidewalk seemed to impede
their progress.

Exactly, you said. *Phragmites australis,*
non-native, invasive.

I get it now, dear husband,
the marsh-usurper fooled me.
Beauty does that to us. And we all fall for it.
Don't we?

Work in Progress

*Two people together is a work heroic in its
ordinariness.*—Adrienne Rich

You're not listening to me, he says
because I'm not agreeing with him and I'm puzzled

because I've heard everything he's said about the grass
and not cutting it today but tomorrow a much better day.

But is it? And how does he know?

But, I say, I have the time to cut the grass and need I say
the inclination because both are necessary: time, inclination

and where will both be if I wait until tomorrow
and what's it to him anyway, today or tomorrow?

But the look in his eyes like I've hurt him, disrespected him,
tells me there's more to this back and forth of ours than grass,

mowing, the level of sun and the way the earth turns on its axis
to bring us tomorrow you can count on it, time passing, the sun rising

whether we see it or not, whether he can estimate respect
or disrespect in my insistence that today is the day

this woman cuts the grass, the desire to try the new mower strong
in me, stronger than his doubt that cutting the grass

will achieve the success I imagine, but what the hell, it's only grass
and who measures success by the length or lack of it of grass?

I mow the lawn and I respect him although he doubts it,
his doubt caught in his throat like that piece of pork

weighting his fork last night that he put into his mouth anyway
and chewed and chewed I could hear his teeth meshing

it took a while but he got it down like this work we do together
so ordinary yet heroic.

Intermission at Symphony Hall

A woman two rows ahead works her fingers
through her husband's white hair, patting it down,
roughing it up again, her fingers in constant contact
with his skin. He doesn't move
or brush her hand away, just stares
at the empty stage.

I know this woman and I don't know her,
the desire simply to be normal, go to a concert,
the hope that music will get through the barriers
his brain has put up,

he who used to play the violin after dinner,
his favorite Mozart quartet on the stereo
and the look on his face like one hundred virgins
have greeted him in heaven. Only he hasn't
touched his instrument in several years, not
since the stroke, the diagnosis of Alzheimer's,
the fall that left him paralyzed on one side,
the cancer slowly taking over his glands.

Any of the above
for it's not as simple as boredom
the stiffness in his shoulders,
the way he holds his head like one of the statues
ranged along the upper tier of the hall,
Greek gods and heroes impervious to music.

Sometimes your future presents itself
right in front of you and it is scary as hell
in this case a man like stone and a woman
so devoted to him that her hands create a symphony
of their life together, the nights of love, the mornings
spent late in bed they couldn't get enough of each other

and his saying what she'll never forget
I love to be caressed.

Boca Chica, Florida

Pelicans cruise the shallows, vying with snorkelers
face-down and bubbling among the kelp.
Practicing avoidance, the pelicans seem intent
on who gets first dibs on the minnows.
The two men I'm with, my husband, his brother,
chat about their absent brother, detailing
his wife's faults, her demands keeping him bound
to her side, away from them. They're hard on her.

A sudden squall revs up for a wild spill of rain.
The shower pleasures the men. Its coolness, they say,
feels rather nice on their upper bodies, their arms.
For me, the shower is an annoying trickle
down my neck, a soaked shirt.

At least grant me a rainbow's audacious bands.
I deplore this sorry beach with its soda cans
snagged in sea weed tentacles, a child's pink plastic shoe
littering the tide-line. *A tropical storm*, Tim says,
its aftermath. He waves his arm
to include ocean, clouds, detritus.
                                    What did you expect?

We're stopped by a downed tree limb,
a cormorant on its tip, beak into the wind, wings
spread out like split halves of an umbrella.
Ruddy turnstones line up behind him, perched
in an orderly row. The birds amuse us, but I think
they're wind-battered, huddled close
for simple comfort.

Leaving, we laugh at the pick-up parked
on Boca Chica Road where everyone can ogle
its flattened tires and crunched fenders, the hunk of cement

in its bed, the hand-painted sign on its hood
proclaiming *Free.*

The Moth Man

In federal prison in West Virginia,
the gimpy old man collects moths attracted by prison lights,
never turned off. Insects swarm
on the beams; bodies pile up.
What he doesn't scavenge,
other prisoners bring to him:

Wild silk moths,
Modest Sphinx moths,
Tiger moths.

Let loose on the internet, he identifies them
and adds them to his collection:
Scarlet-winged Lichen Moths,
Owlet Moths,
Hawkmoths.

In his life outside, he is—or was—
a passionate birder. He's also a pedophile.
Children irresistible, *but,*
he protests,
   I never touched them.

His age shields him from other felons—
big city dealers, assorted crooks, gangsters
with spooky tattoos snaking from wrist to bicep.

What sport in beating on an old man?

Hey Moth-Man,
take a look at this one: black and blue eyespots
on its hind wings.

Human nature, someone once said,
is profoundly phototropic.

Turning towards the light, we can't help it.

Gospel Sing, Key West

for Cathy and Tim

Two streams of women, a few men,
African sashes flowing magenta and bronze
down their backs, over their prodigious chests.
slowly sway down the rows, singing
            Joy is mine today.

As we rise to sing, I feel my hips, my wrists,
my arms pumping in and out, my body surprised
into tribal rhythms I'd forgotten I knew.
Is this what I've come for? The gospel singing
so bold and generous maybe it's true.

They spread across the stage singing
            Peace is mine today
as two undulant lines claim victory again.

I can't believe they're part of Key West, destination
of cruise ships, drug runners, and rafts of Cuban refugees.
Where Duval Street throbs with tourists, body parts
pierced or exposed.

            Satan, get thee behind,
their voices add to the cacophony I can't resist.
Gospel rhythms pulling me up, I embrace the lure
of this tropic city, so decadent and exquisite
with its bougainvillea and hibiscus, air so soft
I want to draw it around me like a scarf.

Atalanta, or the Audacity of Speed

after Ovid

At dusk, I can hear his roar
and a shiver flows down my spine.

Apple of shining gold, when you suddenly appeared
rolling on the path before me, I plucked you from the dust
and continued running
though I could hear him
close behind me,
the ferocity of his breath.

But you were in my palm, like the sun itself,
my bare feet skimming over stones in the rutted path.
Then, your double appeared
asking to find its place, the satisfying balance
of its weight, and too soon the third
rolling beside the track
and his feet drawing closer,
his breath on my neck, his arms claiming his bride
as I stumbled.

I could feel the fine hairs on his chest,
my shoulders and back pressed to the earth.
And when the shrill cheeps
of awakening birds opened the morning,
the gods saw and he bulked up into a lion
and my teeth sharpened,
flexed claws where fingers used to be.

Three

Beyond Ruin

Talus

In the Sangre de Cristos, Katherine and I
scramble over an old avalanche of rocks, game
for a morning hike, our memories flung out
and catching.

In the story Katherine tells, she's lied
to a boy she loves, and he's too young and smitten
to have doubts about her hiking skills.
When she trips and falls three hundred feet
onto the talus, head gashed, ankle broken,
death assumes a face.

Her boyfriend runs for help.

Struggling between despair and calm,
she listens to the warm buzz of insects.
The scent of juniper swells in the sun.
As death leans over her, resistance worms back
through her bones, entering her spine.

Now her memory is my memory
as if I were the fallen one, exposed to the sun,
to ravens cruising the canyons.
Her boyfriend would return, wouldn't he?

I remember hurtling down the hill
on my bike, hitting a car broadside and flying over the top.
I never felt so fully alive, so fully myself

and no one else, if only for a moment
voyaging outside of life,
returning for more.

Making Tracks

Footsteps pock the wet sand, the beach
stamped as if some hero has just passed.
Like a child avoiding sidewalk cracks, I veer
around them. Unlike the sea, its certain return
smoothing everything in its path.

Some tracks intersect, the bold cuts of Nike
meeting Reebok, intricate patterns like my cat's bandit-mask
which I trace with my fingertips. Then her white belly,
her perfect white paws. When she flops on the rug
for a massage, I lean my head into her fur.

In this photo of my mid-twenties self,
I'm sitting on the kitchen chair, a tortoise-shell cat
in my lap. Its front paws extend across my thighs
to keep me attached to a world shrunken back
to my father's kitchen.

He's wifeless and out of sight, standing at the stove
waiting for the pot to boil. I gaze down, intent on the cat.
The doorway promises an escape from linoleum floors,
plastic tablecloths, the grief of an old man with cigar breath,
destined for lung cancer or a heart attack—or both.

I study the angle of my arms, the sleeveless white blouse,
pewter wishbone pinned just above my left breast.
How I wished for a life with the shining grace of that swerve,
a destiny forked and unpredictable. How I stiffened
my resolve, then spilled the cat on the floor.

Night Crossing

I'm a woman driving alone
on a mountain road, following alongside a river
as it plunges down the slope, all nervy restless energy:
furious at rocks blocking its way, at blow-downs
that shift its rage into a chute of acceleration.

Any minute now, the truck barreling
straight for my rear will pass me on a curve
doing sixty. There is thunder in it and darkness,
that alluvial bed. No, that's a stomping upstairs
from a cellar deep in a house I called home, footsteps
like the rapid beating of a heart clocking its survival,
my head resting on a pillow, my ear
thrumming the blood pulse.

Ahead of me, someone's taillights
sucked into the fog like the hiss of an in-taken breath
or is that my own fear, a curse at the back of my throat,
tiredness in my hands, my arms, edging down
into my lower back.

The truck won't go away
nor the night sounds: tires thumping, the radio voices
keeping me company. With the whoosh of his draft,
the truck passes and I cruise through forests
where moose prowl, foraging in the undergrowth,
only to lumber onto the highway for brief encounters.

Beware their kiss, I tell myself, as I scan slopes
of dark spruce and birches that gleam
like invitations on fine white paper.

Mozart at Seventeen

I'd done it again: locked out of my car
that evening after the concert.
No friendly red salute as I flicked the unlock icon.

No keys and my stupid car remained indifferent
while I made the dreaded phone call
to my husband with the news

and could he come to the rescue.
The only bright thing that night was the symphony
Mozart composed at seventeen,

the year his father brought him to Vienna
to seek a position in the court of Empress Maria Theresa.
Only Salieri had won the keys to the court

and there was nothing for Amadeus.
So what does he do?
He attends the symphonies of Haydn,

glorious and inventive,
and over a period of weeks produces a music
filled with restless, angular melodies,

the oboe and flute freed into colorful bursts
that force the violins to yield. Only in the andante
does he settle into more introverted passions.

He was a teenager after all, destined
to trump Salieri, some say even Haydn.
Though he doesn't know this at the time.

Maybe suspects it, so that three centuries later
as I was walking towards my car one evening
after a concert, fishing for my keys,

Mozart seemed to whisper: *In clarity lies the serene.*

Sluice

Yesterday's storm flings itself at Labrador,
leaving us with trees splayed across the road.
We step over broken limbs, ambling towards
the millionaire's cabin and its wild running brook.
No one's home, and we do no harm
standing on the bridge, water cascading below
to calm, unhurried pools.

The cabin commands its rise, an army of trees
sheltering its seclusion, windows shuttered.
Goldilocks would enter and sample the porridge,
the beds. We're content with the hermit thrush
trilling its song from the canopy, calling to its mate.
Wind sifts through the trees like a woman reaching up
to part her husband's hair with her fingers.

Each day a piece of your memory sluices off
like those Greenland glaciers calving. Someday,
I may hike this trail alone. But not today.
Pity we didn't think to film our life together,
even the moment we enter a cloud of black flies,
flailing them like athletes doing jumping jacks.
No matter: the brook obeys its laws, clear water
splashing over rocks. The anemone blooms low
in the bush. As if on cue, you bend to admire it.

The Blue Tent

Two miles up from the nearest road, we collapse
at the edge of a lake, lungs and hearts stretched
almost to the breaking, the trail steeper and more rough
than we'd imagined. Resting, we trade theories
about the audacious blue tent being dismantled
on the opposite shore.

Clouds bloom up white and friendly
while we watch two figures move toward us,
backpacks rising above their heads, their tent scrunched
and stuffed. At first, they are simply color:
a slow red shirt, beige shorts.

As they move closer, we see a man
and a woman. He walks with two canes, stops
often, lurches ahead. She pauses with him,
as if the journey were old and eternal
and they were two Buddhist monks, no destination in mind,
no haste, just the journey and its conversations
about the nature of time, the pleasures of dawn
and morning coffee on the mountain.

Descending, they float over boulders and stout blow-downs
as if the angels of the trail were on alert
making cushions for their boots, the gentleman of two canes
waving them away as he digs in and vaults from precipice
to precipice, his mate running to catch up.

Self-Portrait with Bell's Palsy

for Stephanie Cole

In her studio, she takes her face's slouch
as subject, propping a mirror

to the side of her easel
so she can capture this oddity

in charcoal,

her eye wandering down
to visit her mouth

like the women Picasso painted,
forehead going one way, chin

another: asymmetric beauties.
She seems to be chewing something tough

on the right side
while her left leans into a smile.

For her, the droop in her mouth
and eye is strange and compelling

as the beach glass she collects,
an arrangement of exquisite fragments.

She tacks her image
beside them on the wall,

a woman beyond ruin.

The Day Pavarotti Died

On the locker room's speakers,
Luciano Pavarotti, his soaring, dulcet tenor familiar
as the shiny black lapels expanding over his white shirt,
the limp white hankie he flourishes to mop his brow.
Despite the whining of my hair dryer, the thrill of him
is as present as the sweaty, red-faced woman entering
after her workout. I don't know her name,
only that she's a nurse in her fifties—fit body,
every muscle defined.

During Pavarotti's tender diminuendo
she informs me, *He died of pancreatic cancer.*
That's how my husband died.
Murmuring, *It's a terrible way to die,*
she dumps her gym bag in a dressing room,
pulls the door closed.

I thought she was just another locker-room pal,
sharing a mirror, hair-gel, an obsession
with calories burned, crunches, aerobics, the elliptical machine.
Now I know she's working out her grief
every day, willing it to shrink.

Winter Visit to the D. H. Lawrence Ranch

Taos, New Mexico

My husband didn't want to do this
and the silence between us
is so chill I can snap it between my teeth
like a sliver of ice.

We park and trek uphill
through new-fallen snow,
inserting our boots into footprints
of other pilgrims.

I bow my head at the sepulcher,
Lawrence's ashes in a white tomb.
Ah Lorenzo, you told Frieda
to bury you here

and something of your soul remains
in this air we breathe. Taos pleased you
for a while—the dry, summer heat,
the great light, the Indians and their rituals.

May your spirit be with us now.
Because you drew me here
to this outpost and I'm about to fall off the edge.
Because I'm being tested.

Because it tested you and you flourished.
Because you battled with Frieda
and both of you came through, victorious.
Because no pilgrim can resist looking west

where the desert stretches into boundlessness.
Look, my husband says, *an eagle,*

his eyes discerning the raptor
from the angle of flight, the sheer height

as it floats from mountain slope
to cruise the nearest arroyo, the undersides
of its wings catching light, his voice thrilled,
his hand on my shoulder, our hearts swept clear.

Bosque del Apache, New Mexico

For the Bosque del Apache
we've lugged scopes and binoculars
to this most beautiful of wildlife sanctuaries,
its backdrop of mountains drifting towards the sky.
We drive alongside canals dug to keep fertile the rich farmland.
If we're lucky, we'll see snow geese wintering.

On his tribal lands, it's hard not to think
about Geronimo, captured, finally, and shipped off
to Florida. Resisting to the end, he died of pneumonia,
the old man's disease. We like to remember him fierce.
His usurpers, the ranchers, made their mark
for a while. The government made recompense: these acres,
this sanctuary open to nothing but sky and birds:
cormorants, pin-tail ducks, marsh hawks.

The harvest over, they feast on remnants of corn,
wheat berries, alfalfa. We're content to do nothing
but sit and watch snow geese preen and court.
Mainly they feed, their trip from the Arctic much longer
than ours to get here, more arduous and wired into their brains
for millennia. When a sharp-shinned hawk ventures too close,
the snow geese lift off and we follow them
as the flock shapes and reshapes itself.

No one gets left behind.

Kayaking the Sakonnet

This is what I remember. Heat.
A river. Lugging the kayaks to the beach.
Pushing off. Then paddling out
ahead of my husband, wanting it more than he,
that feeling of buoyancy.

This is what freedom feels like, I thought,
and embraced it all, even the fisherman
calling me over to view six stripers
as long as his arm. He was a fool
but I liked him, liked his success, his need to share it.
Could he see that I too was full of life?

My husband had pulled away. I followed,
passing close to a jumble of rocks
where cormorants spread their wings to dry.
I smiled at the little black crucifixes.
Nothing in this world seemed only one thing
and not another. Witness the jelly fish floating
pink and blowsy as peonies. Yes,
there was a shoal with waves striking
against spiky rocks—something to avoid,

as my husband, the cautious one, warned.
A shoal is a shoal. Nasty to boats.
But I couldn't resist
dipping into its seaweed necklace, a coppery mulch
with a scent of drenched leather.
It followed us home.

A Moving Figure

Retired, my father strolls to the beach,
Quincy Bay shimmering at the end of the block,
flush with sails and the Boston skyline in the distance.
Squantum juts out, a flyover for planes descending to Logan,
my father a moving figure down below, a beach towel
tucked under his arm, a cigar clamped between his teeth,
no hat, no sun screen, his bald pate tanned, his chest
and legs a ruddy brown.

Fear of the ship resting on the shore, its hull split open.
Fear of being that open.

When he enters the water, his cigar set firmly
between his teeth, he flips on his back and floats,
the cigar pointing toward heaven, the waves gentle
as they heave his body up and down the swells.

My brother at the Dead Sea,
not knowing any better, decides to dive in.
As if he were at the neighborhood beach
he strips to his trunks, removes his hearing aid
and foots it quickly to the shore. The others call
to him: "Don't, Richard! Stop!"

A novice, I travel the width of the pool, then the length,
graduating to what I wanted all along: another world
inside my frigid Boston, a warm intrepid inversion
I can take with me into the paradoxical snow
and ice of city streets.

Angelus

Watching me, my brother says, *Why bother? Just cut your grass extra
short
in the fall. Let your leaves blow into your neighbor's yard.*

Kind of crass, this brother.

As if there were a bounty to be paid, I gather up yellow leaves, red,
brown.
Either they succumb to my rake or they resist, hard-scrabble.

There's this place out back where decades of leaves have mounded up,
slowly decomposed. From *ashes to ashes from dust to dust.*

Wearing the priest's blotched thumbprint on my forehead. All that
piety!
Even the print that hung in the dim front hall of my parents' house:

a man and a woman pausing for the Angelus *(Hail, Mary),*
the church bells too potent to ignore.

He doffs his hat, holding it midway between wooden shoes and sky.
She folds her hands, bowing her head, a basket at her feet: the food

she has delivered so he can eat, drink, get right back to work.
As the bells toll, their lives expand through time, the sound echoing

then receding. Nobody is watching as she walks home, her basket
lighter,
something she swings as she walks, liking the swoosh of it,

following its arc as she enters the path to the canal, the clean sweep
of water coursing through the valley.

She doesn't know what lies beyond the church steeple on the horizon,
the sound of the bells still ringing in her ears.

If not the Angelus, I feel the juice of my labor in my shoulders and
   arms,
the reach and pull: to gather, to collect. A certain satisfaction

in the massing, a certain disdain for paid labor and leaf-sucking tubes.
Though once indoors, I worry the skin of my hands, still so unlike

my mother's, cracked and worn. For wasn't she washerwoman, cook,
scrubber of floors and sinks? How many times did she press

her index finger on the ridge worn into her forehead, telling her girls
not to frown as she did. *Sing*, she told us. *Play the piano. Be happy.*

On the Strength and Character of the Norway Maple

And that you attract and bear along with your own lofty being
the very pest that will eat the heart out of each and every leaf

extending from your many branches: the winter moth

whose life cycle depends on you, making it coeval or parasitic—
I can't decide which—your leaves this late in May in tatters,

the moths working their way through the entire tree.
Not one leaf escapes

the industry and appetite of the winter moth, its progress
a stunning instance of sheer nastiness.

For what good is done except to feed a craving run amuck
and when the feeding is done,

slender wisps descend almost invisible like spider webs unraveled,
bearing the tiny worm aiming for the earth

while you, stately, impervious, proceed to send forth a new battalion
of leaves as if it mattered not

that your bounteous crop was devoured.
Take that! winter moth. I shall not be abused.

There is more life in me than you can imagine, more skill
and expertise at treeness

like this bond, my darling, that we've built together you and I
grown stronger with your illness . . .

There is no self-pity where the maple lives
no weakening in the fiber of its being because it simply knows

through roots, trunk, limbs, crown what it does well,
meaning life expressed as fullness

the sheer gutsiness of it.

You Should Avoid Young Children

Because they fill their diapers
with reliable ease, sitting on your lap
or spread out on your best mattress.
Guilt is as foreign to them as vichyssoise.

Because they spread sticky fingers
over the piano keys, looking for you
to hoist them onto your lap. They slam
the ivories for the racket they can make.
Re-think your nap.

Because they are blank slates
on which so much waits to be written,
their eyes opened wide to take everything in,
including the lines around your eyes,
the pouches under your chin.

Because they manipulate the controls
on the TV, finger the holes in the electric socket,
stomp the cat's switching tail only to smile
and gaze at you as if you held the keys to joy.

Because you can embrace them, but
you can't bind them. Because they have nothing
to give you—and everything. Because
something loosens when they come around.
Something opens you didn't know was shut.

Bracket Fungus

All I need is a brief glance
at the bracket fungus clinging to our swamp willow
and the day rushes back when joy spilled over
the brim of my cup and my love joined me
for a tramp through the Sunderland woods.
Jutting out from a tree, a fluted growth
like an exotic fan. *A mushroom?* I asked.
He laughed. *None such would bloom on a tree,*
he said, plucking it off, tapping its flesh
hard as wood.

And beautiful. Like him.
Like the way I felt being with him.
He tossed it into the leaves.

Later, his arm behind my shoulder, his knee
drifting into mine, he waits for me to finish
reading the newspaper and tell him what he has done
so wrong I ignore him. My eyes are wet; he can see that.
The tear thing. He hates it.

So he wrote his old girlfriend
and she wrote back. Stupid letter!
It meant nothing, absolutely nothing.

At the open rehearsal, James Levine says to the trumpeter,
Don't be afraid of the power of that blast.
It's wonderful. Strong emotion, non-destructive
strong emotion, also wonderful.

Whirlwind to Job: *Who shut up the sea with doors?*

After the hurricane, our ordinary town beach
becomes Ocean, at home with Titans, waves swelling

and crashing: the roar of it, the foam,
the shrieks of children

as if the waves meant harm, as if they could take you,
rip your feet out from under you,
toss you in a heap on the sand.

Curses

*The dark thought, the shame, the malice / meet them at
the door laughing and invite them in.*—Rumi

May your children turn their backs on you,
your husband abandon you for a millennial in stilettos.
May the IRS find you've cheated on your taxes.
May your nights be filled with attack dreams
so violent you writhe against your pillow
and fall out of bed, fracturing a rib.
May you fall asleep at your desk and lose your job.
May your house be foreclosed and force you to move
to a motel where cockroaches defecate on the walls.
Your sole entertainment is watching them copulate.
No one will ever want to mate with you.
Unable to resist corndogs and pizza, you grow obese.
May the teeth rot in your head, with pain no pills can abate.

May your children call long-distance
and leave hate messages on your voice mail.
May you see your husband emerging from the Alumni Club
with an Amy Adams look-alike, her dress slit to the waist.
May a cab pull up and splash snow-melt all over your legs.
May you catch the flu and lack health-care coverage.
May you spend eight hours on a gurney in the emergency room.
May you lose control of your bladder. May you weep.

And it shall come to pass
that all these curses shall descend upon you
and overtake you. And I will look upon you
without compassion.

Elegy with Seven Swans

September 9, 2001

Two days before the attack, I watched a flock of swans swimming
in the Forest River estuary.

No jet trails of planes become weapons.

I watched those birds so lovely in their form and felt blessed
because I could observe the slope of their necks

as grace notes. The odd number—of no importance—
except for the loosely remembered fact that swans mate for life.

As my swans swam with seemingly no effort, they tilted their heads
like shy maidens of yore, moving in concert

with one another. *Concert*—denoting a smoothness
and a coming together for a common purpose—in their case

foraging in a wash of red and brown sea weed.
In the ballet they choreographed simply by being there and being
   hungry,

seven white shadows rippled and merged.

Later I learned that a woman who lived close by on the estuary
fed them regularly.

So they could be regarded as vagrants dependent on handouts.
This sojourn was for extras.

Whatever their status—vagrants, symbols of the serene—they were
   indifferent
to their effect on the world—on me.

91

And I liked them for their indifference to me or to the horror being readied for its descent.

About the Poet

Claire Keyes is the author of two previous collections of poetry, *The Question of Rapture* and the chapbook *Rising and Falling.* Her poems and reviews have appeared most recently in *Literary Bohemian, Sugar Mule, Oberon, Crab Orchard Review* and *Blackbird.* In addition, she is the author of *The Aesthetics of Power: The Poetry of Adrienne Rich.* She has won the Robert Penn Warren Award from New England Writers as well as a first prize in poetry from *Smartish Pace.* The recipient of a grant in poetry from the Massachusetts Cultural Council, she also received a poetry fellowship from the Wurlitzer Foundation in Taos, New Mexico. Professor emerita at Salem State Uni-versity, she teaches in the university's lifelong learning program and lives in Marblehead, Massachusetts.

CPSIA information can be obtained at www.ICGtesting.com
Printed in the USA
LVOW06s1056021115

460624LV00042B/257/P